PRESSED FLOWERS · AND · LEAVES

12 Charming Seasonal Projects

by Gabriela Delworth

STERLING INNOVATION
An imprint of Sterling Publishing Co., Inc.

New York / London
www.sterlingpublishing.com

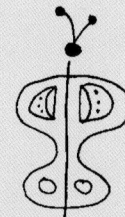

A QUIRK PACKAGING BOOK

© 2011 by Quirk Packaging, Inc.

This 2011 edition published by Sterling Publishing Co., Inc., by arrangement with Quirk Packaging, Inc.
STERLING, the Sterling logo, STERLING INNOVATION, and the Sterling Innovation logo are registered trademarks of Sterling Publishing Co., Inc.

All rights reserved. No part of this publication may be reproduced, stored in a retrieval system, or transmitted, in any form or by any means, electronic, mechanical, photocopying, recording, or otherwise, without prior written permission from the publisher.

This book is part of the *Flower and Leaf Press* kit and is not to be sold separately.

Design and illustrations by Alison Oliver at Sugar
Photography by Mark A. Gore
Cover photography © Lucato, Nancy Nehring, Bill Noll, Kryczka, Nic Taylor, and Agalma with iStockphoto
Tag photograph on pages 15, 17, 18, 21, 25, 27, 29, 33, 35, 37, 41, 43, 45, 46 © Cole Vineyard/iStockphoto
Author photo © Edward Lee

Sterling Publishing Co., Inc.
387 Park Avenue South
New York, NY 10016

ISBN: 978-1-4351-2512-4

Printed and bound in China

10 9 8 7 6 5 4 3 2 1

TABLE OF CONTENTS

INTRODUCTION 4
FLOWERS AND LEAVES 5
    Where to Look 5
    When and What to Collect 6
USING THE PRESS 9
STORING DRIED BOTANICALS 10
WORKING WITH DRIED BOTANICALS 11
    Basic Tools 11
    Tips 12

SPRING 13
    Notecard 14
    Shadow Box 16
    Framed Wreath 20

SUMMER 23
    Stickers 24
    Coasters 26
    Garden Journal 28

FALL 31
    Place Cards 32
    Canvas Art 34
    Place Mats 36

WINTER 39
    Season's Greetings Cards 40
    Vintage Ring 42
    Gift Toppers 44

RESOURCES 47

ACKNOWLEDGMENTS/
ABOUT THE AUTHOR 48

INTRODUCTION

Welcome flower and nature lovers! The drying of flowers and leaves has been in practice for medicinal, fragrant, and cosmetic uses since ancient Egyptian times. As flowers were cultivated in abundance in elaborate gardens and greenhouses during the Victorian era, dried flowers and leaves began to be used for decoration.

I was lucky enough to grow up in a home where gardening was a large part of our lives. My mother loved her plants and took great care of them. She taught me how to harvest and press flowers and leaves, and to incorporate them into beautiful objects that adorned our home or were given to loved ones as gifts.

My desire is to share with you my love of botanicals, and to inspire you to create along with me. I will teach you how to correctly use the press that came with this book. I have also designed twelve modern yet simple projects for you to create using your own blooms and foliage. Imagine making pieces that are lovely enough to display at home, such as framed art; stylish enough to wear, such as a ring; elegant enough to entertain with, such as coasters, place cards, and place mats; and meaningful enough to surprise your loved ones with, such as handmade cards. Step-by-step instructions and beautiful photographs accompany each project.

All you need are flowers, leaves, some common tools and materials, and the included press. Let's start pressing and creating!

 — GABRIELA DELWORTH

FLOWERS AND LEAVES

WHERE TO LOOK

One of the great things about pressing botanicals is that the process defies the ephemerality of nature. You can preserve a flower or leaf in its prime, whether it's a cut flower that you received in a bouquet or a leaf you happened upon on a walk. Look for natural inspiration in these places:

Plantings

Your garden, yard, or plant containers are the easiest places to find flowers and leaves for pressing. Plan your garden in advance of the growing season, so you have preferred shapes and colors to incorporate into projects.

Fallen Foliage

Federal, state, and local parks and forests often prohibit the picking of wildflowers in order to preserve endangered species and ecosystems, so be mindful of these laws. On the other hand, fallen leaves or things that are unattached (don't need to be picked) are for the taking.

Cut Flowers

If you received flowers as a gift, pressing is a great way to extend their beauty and a memory. Buying cut flowers is an expensive alternative to using things you've grown or found, but if you are looking for a specific color or shape, it is an option.

WHEN AND WHAT TO COLLECT

Flowers and leaves can be collected year-round, weather and climate permitting. Here are some general guidelines when gathering potential pressings:

※ Harvest flowers in the late morning after the dew has dried, and the flowers begin to open.

※ Pick flowers and leaves not only at their peak but also at different stages of development for variety.

※ Look for well-shaped flowers and leaves without any damage; drying will only emphasize flaws.

※ Keep color selection in mind when choosing flowers: bright colors (blue, yellow, orange) stay relatively the same color; dark ones (red, purple) tend to turn even darker; whites often turn tan; and pastels (pink, lavender) may fade.

※ For best results, press your blooms and foliage as soon as you collect them.

Flowers

The easiest flowers to press are those that are naturally flat (since a press flattens them further) and without much moisture (the faster a flower dries, the better it retains color and shape). Here's a list of flowers that are ideal for pressing:

- alyssum
- anemone
- aster
- azalea
- baby's breath
- begonia
- bleeding heart
- buttercup
- butterfly weed
- cockscomb
- columbine
- cornflower or bachelor's button
- cosmos
- crocus
- delphinium or larkspur
- dogwood
- Dutchman's-breeches
- English daisy
- geranium
- goldenrod
- heather
- Johnny-jump-up
- lily-of-the-valley
- nemesia
- phlox
- pansy
- poppy
- primrose
- Queen Anne's lace
- salvia
- statice
- sweet pea
- verbena
- violet

Flowers (continued)

Three-dimensional, multi-petal flowers should be sectioned before pressing. For example, if preparing roses, slice them in half lengthwise with a craft knife, then press both halves. Other flowers that need preparation include ageratums, candytufts, carnations, chrysanthemums, dahlias, hydrangeas, marigolds, peonies, and zinnias.

Naturally moist flowers—calla lilies, daffodils, irises, orchids, sunflowers, and tulips—are more likely to form mildew and decay before they dry out. Remove any fleshy stems, stamens, or pistils before pressing, because these parts carry the most moisture.

TIP

Press individual petals for drying success, then reassemble them to make your flower whole.

Leaves

Leaves are naturals when it comes to pressing, and they retain their color well. Just make sure to avoid thick, fleshy leaves. Also, don't limit your leaf choices to the trees in your yard. Look to the leaves of flowers (like roses) and non-flowering plants (like ferns and ivy), too.

Herbs

As with flowers and leaves, herbs that are naturally flat are best suited for pressing. Chamomile, lavender, rosemary, sage, parsley, and even catnip are all excellent options.

TIP

The world of botanicals is vast, so don't be afraid to experiment with flowers, leaves, and herbs that are not listed here.

USING THE PRESS

In order to press your flowers and leaves, you need the wooden boards (for weight), the Velcro straps (for pressure), the corrugated cardboard separators (for ventilation), and the blotting paper (for absorbing moisture). Follow these steps to start pressing:

1. Choose the flowers/leaves that you want to press. Trim any stems that may be too long to fit in the press.

2. Undo the Velcro straps on the press and set them aside.

3. Place a piece of cardboard on top of one of the wooden boards.

4. Place a piece of blotting paper on top of the cardboard.

5. Position your flowers/leaves on the blotting paper, making sure that they do not touch each other.

6. Place another piece of blotting paper on top of your flowers/leaves, followed by another piece of cardboard.

7. Repeat steps 4–6 for multiple layers. There should be 2 pieces of blotting paper between the pieces of cardboard in each layer.

8. Once you have all of your layers, place the second wooden piece on top.

9. Tighten the Velcro straps around your press, making sure that both deliver equal pressure.

10. In a dry spot, keep the flowers/leaves in the press from 2 to 4 weeks. Retighten the straps every day or every other day as they dry.

---------------- *TIP* ----------------
For best pressing, place flowers/leaves of similar thicknesses on the same layer.

STORING DRIED BOTANICALS

There are a number of ways to store your pressings, so you may want to choose one that fits your space or budget. Ideally, you want to keep your dried botanicals away from sunlight and in a cool spot. Here are some storage options:

- In a sealable plastic bag (remove as much air as possible before sealing)
- In a plastic storage container
- In a flat box between layers of tissue paper
- Between acid-free glassine sheets
- In a waxed envelope
- In a phone book or other large tome
- In a CD case
- In your press

TIP

Check your stored botanicals every so often. If you see mold or mildew on a flower or leaf, discard that botanical immediately to prevent the mold from spreading.

WORKING WITH DRIED BOTANICALS

Gathering flowers and leaves for a project is one of my favorite activities; it's when I get to really enjoy my harvest! For the following projects, I used flowers and leaves that I enjoy and that were readily available to me. Feel free to substitute your favorite and/or easily attained blooms and foliage into these projects.

There are no hard-and-fast rules when it comes to selecting the flowers and leaves to use in a project. Though it may seem challenging in the beginning, the more you try out different layouts, the more you will learn what colors, shapes, and textures work best together. Harmony is a very important factor when working on a composition, but also get creative and experiment.

BASIC TOOLS

Here are the basic tools you'll need to handle your pressings and to complete the projects in this book:

❋ **Tweezers:** For handling your delicate dried flowers and leaves.

❋ **Craft brushes in a variety of sizes:** For applying glue to your pressings.

❋ **Ruler:** For measuring; a metal ruler is great for tearing paper against to get a decorative edge.

❋ **Pencil:** For marking measurements.

❋ **Scissors:** For cutting paper.

❋ **Craft knife:** For cutting down flowers and cutting out different sizes of card stock.

- ❋ **White craft or paper glue:** For gluing paper projects.
- ❋ **Glue gun and glue sticks:** For gluing nonporous materials, like plastic.
- ❋ **Clear urethane glue:** For projects in which the glue may show.
- ❋ **Clear sealer:** For protecting dried flowers and leaves with a nice, glass-like finish; it's available in matte or glossy formulas.
- ❋ **Bone folder:** For making sharp, even creases when folding paper.

----------------  ----------------

If you don't have a bone folder, you can run the back of a spoon or your thumbnail along each fold to flatten it smoothly.

TIPS

1. Lay out your project design before permanently adhering pieces.
2. Trim your blooms and foliage to get the sizes and shapes you want.
3. Trim the stems to achieve varying heights of flowers or leaves.
4. Add a touch of paint to faded flowers to enhance their appearance.
5. Highlight dark flowers by combining them with light-colored flowers.

NOTECARD

Many special messages can be conveyed with a card, and a card is even more meaningful if you make it. I always like to keep a nice selection of handmade cards to send out during the year, and I love using pressed flowers and leaves to decorate them. Let's make a card for any occasion!

MATERIALS

* Card stock (Use the card stock that came with your press.)
* Bone folder
* Textured or handmade paper
* Ruler
* Pencil
* Scissors
* White glue
* 3 pansies with stems
* Tweezers
* Craft brush

HOW-TO

1. Fold the piece of card stock in half lengthwise with your bone folder.
2. Measure, mark, and cut out a piece of textured or handmade paper about 3" x 5" (7.5cm x 12.5cm).

TIP: Place the textured paper against a metal ruler and tear it by hand to get a decorative, rough edge.

3. Place some glue on the back of the textured paper rectangle, and press it to the front of the card stock. Make sure it is centered.
4. Evenly line up the bases of the pansies' stems about ½" (13mm) from the bottom edge of the textured paper. Then evenly space the flowers about 1" (2.5cm) apart from each other.
5. Carefully brush glue onto the back of the shortest flower, and press the flower onto the textured paper rectangle. Repeat with the other flowers.
6. Let dry completely before inscribing and sending.

TIP: Decorate the envelope, too!

SPRING

SHADOW BOX

I made this shadow box for a friend who is a gardener. The challenge was filling the box with interesting yet simple things. I chose an old book page with a botanical illustration as the focal point for my layout and made sure to take advantage of the box's depth by creating a 3-D effect with other items.

MATERIALS

* 8½" x 11" x 1½" (21.5cm x 28cm x 4cm) shadow box
* Soft cloth
* Glass cleaner
* 5 old book pages
* White glue
* 8 statice, 9 baby's breath branches, 3 rose leaves, 1 daisy, 3 carnations, 1 cosmos, 2 delphiniums, 1 orchid, 1 orchid bud
* Tweezers
* Glue gun and glue stick
* Decorative paper scraps (colored papers, scrapbooking papers, gift wrap, etc.)

continued >

HOW-TO

1. Remove any dust from the window of your shadow box with a soft cloth and cleaner.

2. Fan the old book pages the width of your shadow box, and glue them together with white glue. Let dry completely.

3. I mimicked the lines of the botanical illustration with 8 statice, 4 baby's breath branches, and 1 rose leaf. Glue the flowers and leaf to the book page with your glue gun.

4. With your paper craft punch and a strip of decorative paper that is at least the width of the book page, make a paper "ribbon," then glue it across the bottom of the front book page with white glue.

5. Center a white daisy on the paper ribbon, brush the back of the flower with white glue, and adhere. Let dry completely.

6. Make a small flower bouquet with 3 carnations, 2 baby's breath branches, and 2 rose leaves, then glue the lower stems of the flowers and leaves and overlap them. Let dry completely.

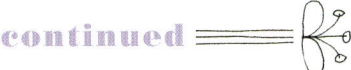

continued

SHADOW BOX (continued)

7. Place the fanned out book pages across the top of your box and secure with a pin.

TIP: Most shadow boxes come with pins, but if yours doesn't, use straight pins. You might need to bend them, depending on the depth of your box.

8. Pin your bouquet onto the fanned out book pages in the upper-left corner.

9. Glue the cosmos and 2 delphiniums directly onto the shadow box in the lower-right corner with your glue gun.

10. To make the banner, measure, mark and cut out a decorative strip of paper, 9" x 1¾" (23cm x 4.5cm). Cut a triangle every 1" (2.5cm) along the strip of paper, cutting up approximately 1¼" (3cm).

11. Fold the uncut ½" (13mm) of the paper strip back and glue the gold cord inside the "casing" with your glue gun.

12. Glue the scrapbooking letters to the banner with white glue, forming the word "garden." Let dry completely.

TIP: If you don't have scrapbooking letters, cut letters from cards you have received or from magazines.

13. Drape the banner across your shadow box, securing both ends of the gold cord with pins.

continued >

* Paper craft punch
* Craft brush
* Ruler
* Pencil
* Scissors
* 11" (28cm) long gold cord
* Scrapbooking letters
* 8½" x 12" (21.5cm x 30.5cm) piece of textured or handmade paper
* Bone folder
* Hole punch
* 5" (12.5cm) long raffia ribbon

14 Fill the lower-left corner of the shadow box with a handmade card: fold the textured paper in half lengthwise with your bone folder.

TIP: Write a message for your recipient inside the handmade card.

15 Punch 2 holes through both layers of the folded paper with your hole punch, ¾" (2cm) from the fold and 2" (5cm) from the top and bottom edges.

16 Tie the raffia ribbon through the 2 holes.

17 Make a paper "ribbon" the width of your card with the paper craft punch and a strip of decorative paper, then glue it across the bottom of the card with white glue.

18 Lay out the orchids and remaining baby's breath on the front of your card, brush the backs of the flowers with white glue, then adhere. Let dry completely.

19 Pin only the bottom layer of the card to the base of the box and close the lid of the shadow box.

SPRING

FRAMED WREATH

Framed botanical art is a very elegant option for decorating a wall. It also makes a great housewarming or wedding gift. Keep your recipient in mind when choosing a color theme, as well as a complementary frame.

MATERIALS

- 11" x 14" (28cm x 35.5cm) sheet of card stock
- Ruler
- Pencil
- 12 filler branches, 12 baby's breath branches, 6 hydrangeas, and 6 delphiniums
- Tweezers
- Glue gun and glue stick
- 11" x 14" (28cm x 35.5cm) frame
- Soft cloth
- Glass cleaner
- 11" x 14" (28cm x 35.5cm) mat with 8" x 10½" (20cm x 26.5cm) opening

HOW-TO

1. Measure 3" (7.5cm) from each side of the card stock and make a mark, then measure 3½" (9cm) from the top and bottom edges of the card stock and make a mark; these marks represent the perimeter of your wreath.

2. In the center of your perimeter, draw a circle with a diameter of about 6½" (16.5cm).

3. Use this circle as the centerline for placing your blooms and branches: layer filler branches, followed by the baby's breath, around the centerline, going in a clockwise direction.

4. Alternate the placement of your hydrangeas and delphiniums on top of the branches, going in a clockwise direction.

TIP: To emphasize the three-dimensionality of this wreath, allow a few sprigs to overlap the mat. For a flatter look, cut the mat evenly all around so the wreath does not touch the mat's edges.

5. Glue the filler branches one by one onto the circle.

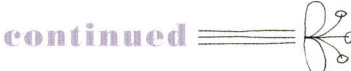
continued

FRAMED WREATH (continued)

6. Repeat step 5 with the baby's breath, hydrangeas, and delphiniums.

7. Before framing your art, clean the glass on both sides, making sure it is clear from any dust.

8. Place your cardstock with your wreath facing down; look on the other side of the glass to make sure it is centered. Replace the backing and mat and secure your frame.

   VARIATION: Get creative when turning your dried botanicals into framed art, whether you choose to feature a single flower, a colorful bouquet, or a collage. Also, have fun with your frame's size and shape, as well as the color of the mat.

STICKERS

When I write letters by hand, I like to seal the envelopes with a pressed flower flourish. These stickers also look great on gift tags or applied to any paper surface that could use a little embellishment. Plus, you get to use those tiny buds or flowers that are otherwise too small to incorporate into other projects.

MATERIALS

- 1 pansy per sticker
- Tweezers
- 1 sheet of clear stickers in any shape or size
- Envelopes or gift tags

HOW-TO

1. Place your pressed flower faceup on your work space.
2. Peel off a sticker and place the sticky side on top of the flower. Make sure the flower is centered, and avoid getting the sticker stuck to your work surface.
3. Lift up the sticker with the flower firmly attached.
4. Place it on your envelope or tag, and press firmly for a few seconds.
5. Repeat steps 1–4 for the rest of your stickers.

TIP: Once you've placed your sticker, set something heavy on top of it to help the sticker adhere to the flower and paper surface.

SUMMER

COASTERS

Summer is chock-full of invitations to outdoor parties and barbecues, and I always like to bring a handmade gift. A set of floral coasters is both beautiful and useful—ideal for resting summer cocktails upon. These coasters are so simple, you can even make them the same day you're giving them!

MATERIALS

* 4" (10cm) clear, round glass coasters
* Soft cloth
* Glass cleaner
* 6 small or 3 large pansies per coaster
* Tweezers
* Craft brush
* Clear urethane glue
* Clear sealer

HOW-TO

1. Wipe your glass coasters with a soft cloth and cleaner to get rid of any dust.

2. These coasters have beveled edges, which guided the placement of the pansies. If your coasters are not beveled, measure in about ½" (13mm). If you are using small pansies, place the 6 blooms in a circle so that their bottommost petals almost touch one another; for larger blooms, place them in a more triangular pattern with their bottommost petals almost touching.

3. Brush a little glue on the glass where your flower will be placed, and press the flower onto the coaster.

4. Repeat step 3 with each flower until your design is finished.

5. Repeat steps 3–4 to complete your set of coasters.

6. Let dry completely.

7. Once dry, brush a coat of sealer over each flower.

8. Let dry completely.

VARIATION: Try gluing your pansies face up on the underside of the coaster, so they look like they're embedded in the glass.

SU
MM
ER

GARDEN JOURNAL

A garden journal is a special place to keep dried flower and leaf samples, garden drawings and plans, notes, seed packets, photos, and stories. It also makes a wonderful personalized gift for any gardener or nature lover.

MATERIALS

- Decorative paper scraps (colored papers, scrapbooking papers, gift wrapping, etc.)
- Ruler
- Pencil
- Scissors
- White glue
- Store-bought journal, approximately 5" x 8¼" (12.5cm x 21cm)
- 6 rose leaves, 2 orchids, and 2 orchid buds
- Tweezers
- Craft brush

HOW-TO

1. From your decorative paper scraps, choose a color that is a nice contrast to the colors of your journal and flowers.

2. Measure, mark, and cut out your decorative paper into a strip about 1¼" x 8¼" (3cm x 21cm), or in a similar proportion to the size of your journal.

3. Place glue on the back of your decorative paper strip, and press it to the front cover of your journal about ½" (13mm) from the right edge.

4. Let dry completely.

5. Starting at the bottom of the journal, fan out 3 rose leaves on and around the paper strip, going up about 3" (7.5cm).

6. Place the other 3 rose leaves in a similar fashion about ½" (13mm) up from the first set of leaves.

7. Set each of the orchids on the leaves about 1" (2.5cm) apart.

8. Center the 2 orchid buds on the paper strip, starting from the top edge of the journal.

continued

GARDEN JOURNAL (continued)

9. Carefully brush glue on the back of your first leaf, and press it in place on the decorative paper strip.

10. Repeat step 9 for all leaves.

11. Carefully brush glue on the back of your first flower, and press it in place.

12. Repeat step 11 for all flowers and buds.

13. Let dry completely.

TIP: Add some pressed flowers and leaves inside the journal as a surprise!

FALL

PLACE CARDS

Place cards are not only useful for organizing your guests' seating, but they also add a decorative element to your dinner table. And nothing pairs better with a fall feast than the vibrant red of Japanese maple leaves. Their shape is beautiful yet delicate, making them ideal to use on these miniature cards!

MATERIALS

* Card stock
* Ruler
* Pencil
* Scissors or craft knife
* Bone folder
* 1 Japanese maple leaf per card
* Tweezers
* Craft brush
* White glue
* Fine black marker

HOW-TO

1. Measure, mark, and cut out your place cards from card stock. Each card should be 3½" x 4" (8.5cm x 10cm).

2. Fold each card in half widthwise with your bone folder.

3. Place each leaf on the left side of the card at a 45-degree angle.

4. Gently brush the back of your first Japanese maple leaf with glue, and press it onto the card.

5. Repeat step 4 to make as many place cards as you need.

6. Let dry completely.

7. Neatly handwrite the names of your guests in the open spaces on the cards.

VARIATION: Choose a thin ribbon in a color that complements your Japanese maple leaves, cut it the width of your cards, and glue it across the bottom of each.

CANVAS ART

Pre-stretched canvas is one my favorite framing alternatives. It's simple, inexpensive, durable, and the perfect backdrop for a leaf *objet d'art*. Try a minimal composition like this pair or fill a canvas with a brimming collage. There's no frame stopping you!

MATERIALS

- 2 gingko or 4 autumn teardrops, depending on which canvas you make
- 8" x 10" (20cm x 25.5cm) pre-stretched canvas
- Tweezers
- Craft brush
- White glue

HOW-TO

1a For the gingko leaves (left canvas), line up the bases of the stems about 3" (7.5cm) from the bottom edge of the canvas. The leaves' blades should be about 2½" (6.5cm) from the side edges of the canvas.

1b For the autumn teardrops (right canvas), line up the bases of the stems about 3½" (9cm) from the bottom edge of the canvas. The leftmost and rightmost leaves' blades should be about ¾" (2cm) from the side edges of the canvas.

2 Gently brush the back of the leftmost leaf with glue, and press the leaf onto your canvas.

3 Repeat step 2 for the rest of your leaves.

4 Let dry completely.

TIP: Decorate a few canvases in different sizes and group them together on a wall.

FALL

PLACE MATS

Place mats are a simple way to bring the rich fall colors of orange, red, yellow, and brown into your décor. As the weather grows cool, gather leaves in various stages of transformation for this project. Mix and match so that no two place mats are alike. Make just one or two to set under a dish of seasonal hors d'oeuvres or a whole set for the dining table. Bon appétit!

MATERIALS

- Textured or handmade paper
- Ruler
- Pencil
- Scissors
- 2 maple and 2 oak leaves (opposite) or 2 maple and 2 ginkgo leaves (page 38) per place mat
- Tweezers
- Craft brush
- White Glue

HOW-TO

1. Measure, mark, and cut out the place mats from textured or handmade paper. Each place mat should be 18" x 14" (45.5cm x 35.5cm).

   TIP: If your paper isn't too thick, place it against a metal ruler and tear it by hand to get a decorative, rough edge.

2. Both designs are very similar and can be constructed the same way: line up the bases of the stems about 5½" (14cm) from the bottom edge of the textured paper. The leftmost and the rightmost leaves' blades should be about 3" (7.5cm) or 3½" (9cm) from the side edges. Evenly space out the middle 2 leaves from there.

   TIP: When selecting leaves for this project, look for pairs in which both individual leaves are close to the same size. The pairs will pop better if their colors and shapes contrast.

3. Gently brush the back of the leftmost leaf with glue, and press the leaf to the paper.

4. Repeat step 3 for the rest of your leaves.

continued

PLACE MATS (continued)

5 Repeat steps 2–4 if making a set of place mats.

6 Let dry completely.

7 After the leaves are dry, brush them with clear sealer for a more finished look.

8 Let dry completely.

TIP: For spill-proof place mats, laminate them using clear self-adhesive laminating sheets or rolls found at any office supplies store. Make sure you smooth out the laminate to prevent wrinkles. You can also take them to a copy shop to have them laminated.

VARIATION: Make a different set of place mats for each season, swapping them out at the spring and fall equinoxes and the summer and winter solstices.

SEASON'S GREETINGS CARDS

Every year, I look forward to making holiday cards. I like to plan my design and start collecting botanicals early in the year to make sure I have enough leaves (and time!) to make a card for everyone on my list.

MATERIALS

* Card stock (Use the card stock that came with your press.)
* Bone folder
* 4 silver lace or 2 cedar leaves, depending on the card you make
* Tweezers
* Craft brush
* White glue
* Silver or red ultra-fine powder glitter, depending on the card you make

HOW-TO

1 Fold the piece of card stock in half lengthwise with your bone folder.

2a For the silver lace (left card), place the leftmost leaf ½" (13mm) from the bottom edge of the card and ¼" (6mm) from the fold. Place the next stem 1½" (4cm), the third one 2" (5cm), and the rightmost one 2½" (6.5cm) from the bottom edge. The leaves should almost be touching one another.

2b For the cedar leaves (right card), place the bases of the stems 2½" (6.5cm) from the bottom edge of the card. Overlap the leaves in order to fit them onto the card.

3 Carefully brush the back of the leftmost leaf with glue, and press it onto your card stock. Repeat with the rest of your leaves.

4 Let dry completely.

5 Brush a thin layer of glue over the blades of the silver lace, then sprinkle silver glitter over the glue for a shimmery, snowy effect. To give the cedar leaves "ornaments," strategically dab dots of glue on the leaves, then sprinkle the red glitter, aiming for the dabs.

TIP: Use a glitter shaker to sprinkle glitter evenly.

6 Let dry completely.

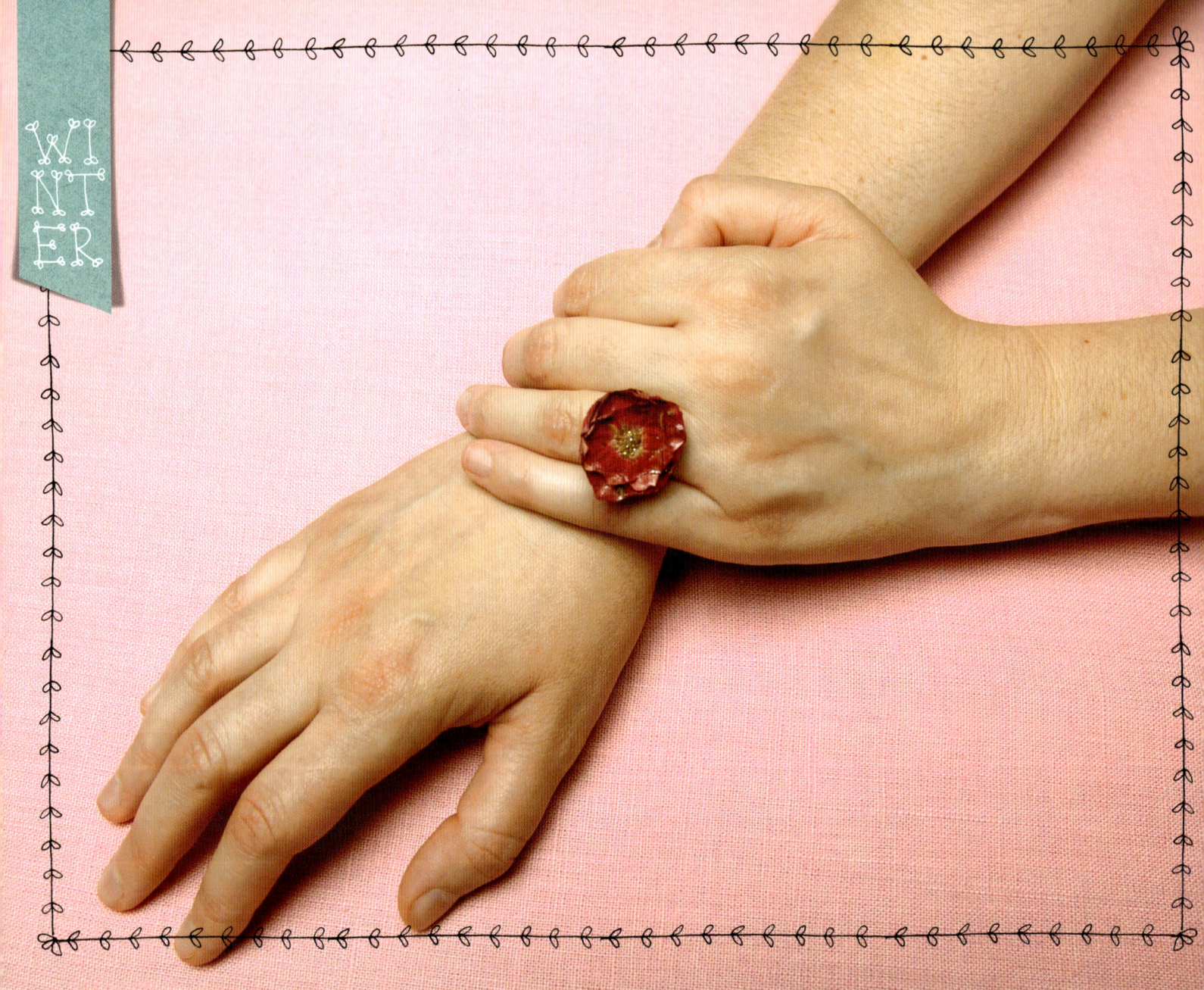

VINTAGE RING

I always try to keep an interesting collection of adornments and pieces in my studio to incorporate into projects. While searching for inspiration, a vintage ring caught my eye and I immediately knew I wanted to design a fabulous piece of jewelry using pressed flowers.

MATERIALS

- Soft cloth
- Vintage ring
- Paper
- 3 or 4 rose petals of varying sizes
- Clear sealer
- Craft brush
- Gold ultra-fine powder glitter
- Clear urethane glue

HOW-TO

1. Clean any dust from the ring with a soft cloth.
2. Brush each pressed rose petal with sealer, and let dry completely. It should dry clear and hard with a glass-like finish.
3. Once dry, brush a second coat of sealer on the petals, then sprinkle them with a dusting of glitter.

TIP: Sprinkle the center of the smallest petal with a clump of glitter to replicate the look of a flower; the smallest petal will be the focal point of your ring.

---

4. Let dry completely.
5. Glue the flowers on top of each other with a small drop of glue on each petal, layering the largest on bottom to the smallest on top.
6. Let dry completely.
7. Place a small drop of clear urethane glue on the center of the ring's setting, then gently press your layered petals onto it.
8. Let dry completely.

GIFT TOPPERS

Gift styling has always been one of my passions, and I find that gift toppers really dress up a package. When wrapping a present for a gardener or nature lover, I always like to include pressed flowers and leaves.

MATERIALS

- 2 cedar, 1 silver lace, and 1 petite licorice
- Tweezers
- Glue gun and glue stick
- 5" (12.5cm) long ¼" (6mm) wide satin ribbon
- Double-sided tape

BRANCH BOUQUET
HOW-TO

1. Look for branches that are uniform in size, or cut them so they are similar in size.
2. Layer the branches, starting with the 2 cedar branches on the bottom and the silver lace and petite licorice fanned out on top.
3. Glue the lower stems of the leaves, then overlap them.
4. Let dry completely.
5. Tie the ribbon in a neat bow, and glue it on top of the overlapped stems.
6. Let dry completely.
7. Adhere the topper to the package with double-sided tape.

TIP: Either let your gift wrap influence your flower and leaf choices, or choose a gift wrap that complements your already-made topper.

continued

GIFT TOPPERS (continued)

MATERIALS

- Card stock
- Ruler
- Pencil
- Scissors
- 11 rose leaves and 6 baby's breath branches
- Tweezers
- Glue gun and glue stick
- Double-sided tape

MINI WREATH
HOW-TO

1. Draw a small circle about 2" (5cm) in diameter on the card stock and cut it out.
2. Layer the rose leaves around the edge of the circle, going in a clockwise direction; two-thirds of each leaf should hang off the edge of the paper circle. Now lay the baby's breath in the center of the leaves, going in a clockwise direction.
3. Glue the rose leaves one by one all the way around the edge of the circle.
4. Glue the stalks of baby's breath one by one on top of the rose leaves.
5. Let dry completely.
6. Adhere the topper to the package with double-sided tape.

TIP: Write your gift recipient's name in the center of the wreath!

RESOURCES

CRAFT SUPPLIES
A. C. Moore
acmoore.com

Jo-ann Fabric and Craft Stores
joann.com

GLUE AND GLITTER
iLoveToCreate
ilovetocreate.com

SCISSORS
Fiskars
fiskars.com

SHADOW BOX
Martha Stewart
marthastewart.com

PAPER CRAFT PUNCHES
Martha Stewart
marthastewart.com

VINTAGE JEWELRY
Way to Bead
etsy.com/shop/waytobead

PRE-PRESSED FLOWERS AND LEAVES
Nature's Pressed, Inc.
naturespressed.com

FAVORITE BOOKS
Handmade Christmas
by Martha Stewart Living Magazine

Fanciful Paper Flowers
by Sandra Evertson

Sara Lugg's The Handcrafted Wedding
by Sarah Lugg

FAVORITE BLOGS
Martha Stewart's the Crafts Dept.
thecraftsdept.marthastewart.com

Holiday with Matthew Mead
holidaywithmatthewmead.com

Marie Claire Idées
mci.blogs.marieclaireidees.com

THANKS

To my mother, Gladys, for inspiring, providing, and teaching me with the tools of creativity since my early days.

To my late Dad and Mirta and Julia for listening to my dreams and supporting me along the way, thanks for being there…always. And thanks to Ed, my lovely man, for all your patience, support, and numerous trips to stores to pick up supplies. And for believing in me.

Thanks to Sharyn Rosart, designer Alison Oliver, and everyone at Quirk Packaging, and to Devorah Klein and Betsy Beier at Sterling Publishing who have made this project possible. And a special thanks to my editor, Erin Canning, for her consideration, help, and patience.

ABOUT THE AUTHOR

Gabriela Delworth designs products, projects and tutorials for leading arts-and-crafts manufacturers. She also writes articles and does photography for national and international publications in print and online, and her projects are often featured on national television segments in Canada. She teaches a variety of classes and workshops in Canada and abroad. She lives in Toronto. Visit her website at www.gabrieladelworth.com.